Secret Keys

Secret Keys

Melody Starr

Rev. date: 06/21/2016

To order additional copies of this book, contact:
Xlibris
1-888-795-4274
www.Xlibris.com
Orders@Xlibris.com
742662

Contents

The Perfect Place For You

As I hold your hand
Your final day alive
I tried to control my tears
And forced to see the other side.

Where the sky reached the limit
And you close your eyes in peace
Where protection comes so easy
With no need to worry.

I felt relieved at the fact
That your suffering was through
I smiled because I knew
Heaven would be the perfect for you.

Nothing can touch you
I can get a good sleep
And I know you didn't regret
The day you were set free.

When God whispered your name
Everyone else never knew
But, we shared a special secret
Heaven was the perfect place for you.

Some people who lost a loved one
This is for all of you
Who don't know already
There's a perfect place for you too!

You will make it shine
And someday take me with you
I'll always be looking up
At the perfect place for you.

You Already Left

As your walking towards the door
I ask why you walk so slow
because as far as i'm concerned
you left me long ago.

We already crossed that bridge
I've been walking the path alone
ever since you started to ignoreme
i'm used to it by now.

My hearts already broken
You don't even know how
either way i'm alone
so why are you just leaving now?

I've already felt alone
I've already felt the pain
so, if you were to leave me now
I would feel the same.

Why would you stick around?
It's just like having you here
You won't give me affection
or give me attention.

And without those things
i'm still in need
You just walk away
But, i'll never be free.

It's Just Pride

Your standing in front of me
with shock in your eyes
due to the fact that
I'm not giving you another try.

I keep a straight face
I really have to try
because if I fumble
you'll know it's just my pride.

Inside I feel so weak
like I'm telling you a lie
when my heart is sinking
my pride tells you goodbye.

It should feel right
like I'm doing the right thing
my pride makes me tell things
that my heart doesn't mean.

That's why I'm not happy
even if for my own good
I wish I could feel that way
but, I understood.

If you hear my voice struggle
that's the real me
but, I'll never tell you
how I'm really feeling.

Just as you walk away
I show my real side
because that's the way I feel
not my pride.

Deep inside, there's a broken heart
I have to push aside
My pride will move on
now, I just have to try.

Four Walls

These four walls I see,
completely understand.
They know me better
than anyone else can.

They ask no questions.
They leave me be.
When I hide,
they cover me.

The silence never breaks.
I'm comfortable with that.
When I would make a mistake,
these walls would never laugh.

I can be anyone
even a little shy.
This is exactly what I want
when I have a good cry.

The outside world can go to hell.
I want to be alone.
These four walls,
my home sweet home.

Vacation

I walk to the bathroom mirror.
Say what I always say.
"The nice girls is taking a vacation,
and it's starting today.

I've always treated people,
with perfect charm.
Had a sweet approach,
but off went the alarms.

There were so many times,
I got shot down.
I took it hard.
Fell down with no sound.

But, I said it would be different.
Turns out I wasn't that brave.
Letting people walk on me,
being a good slave.

My personality holding me,
against my will.
I want people to like me,
so i'll only spill.

When the blinds are pulled down,
my true self hate,
built up inside.
It's already too late.

I want to scream so loud.
I don't get back my respect,
when I give it out.
Many nights, I haven't slept.

I want to rebel.
Cast a spell,
upon myself, to give them hell.

But, in some small way,
I get to be me.
Just not the part of me,
I want to be.

Common Sense

You walked out even though,
you knew what you had.
Saw what else was out there,
but I know you'll be back.

I don't know why you made this move,
you and me were perfect.
We had a good shot at love,
and we deserved it.

Some girl warped your mind,
that you didn't need me.
It's not going to work.
You still have our keys.

You know I'm good for you,
so I don't need a plan.
It won't take very long,
to turn around and follow the tracks.

So, just regain your common sense,
and believe our love is real.
I have the heart of both of us,
that she can never steal.

When you come to your senses,
just give me a call.
We taught each other that,
love conquers all.

Keep It

You gave my heart back.
You didn't want it anymore
well, neither do I
I want you to have it.

I thought it was safe in your hands
maybe it still will be
I accept that were over
This is not to make you feel guilty.

It would make no sense to keep it
It's just no use
I won't be needing it anymore
This is what I choose.

You can bury my heart in your yard
or tuck it in a drawer
be as careless with it as I was
because there is no one else it would be for.

I don't have any plans
but, I'm sure you do.
This is my heart
that I'm giving back to you.

All the good times that you won't look at
are all supplied in here
You won't have to look back again
but, it will be near.

Do with it what you want
tuck it in a safe place
or let it collect dust
keep it either way.

Before The Sun Rises

I look around this place
there was nobody I knew
My eyes were getting tired
until they came across you.

I rose from my seat
boy, I'm on my way
better snatch you quick
todays our lucky day.

Come on, lets take a walk
before the sun rises
kiss me while the starts are out
forget what time it is.

There is no tomorrow
no time to distract
save them for other days
because this one won't last.

Will there be more after tonight?
we will soon see my dear
After the kiss goodnight
will it end with a tear?

Well, let me reassure you
I kind of like the idea
of one mysterious night
but, maybe I will see ya.

Everyday could be
just as this night.
We should have more than one
and we could be alright.

So, give me a call
lets book another fling
when we like each other
we can do anything.

Backyard

I am subconscious
with open eyes
looking at stars
that resemble my eyes.

My setting is freedom
an open space
somewhere I landed
I know this place.

My vision as close as I want it
right in my backyard
I'm on a blanket in the grass
with dreams in my heart.

The night is spirited
this isn't pretend
my dreams are the best
I won't settle or bend.

I'm ready for a happening.
I know there is a cause
for dreams to be so particular
for each individual abroad.

There is impatience sometimes
it's a little tough
like i'm still young
but, times almost up.

But in my confidence
it'll happen when it's meant to
have memories of waiting
for one to come true.

Fate is still on it's way
and it just might
happen in my backyard
so, I will look with pealed eyes.

When my vision comes to life
I only use to take a glimpse
seems I've been waiting since I was ten
been here ever since.

Such a good feeling to dream
when they're still in my heart
and i'll be patient
here in my backyard.

Frozen

I'm falling asleep on wet pillows
that won't have a chance to dry.
Because he has chose someone else
and now, he just passes me by.

When I thought love wasn't for me
It wasn't in the cards
you made me a believer
but now, you're so far.

I'm as dead as flowers in winter
frozen to the bone.
And the suns not warm enough
to put color in my tone.

To love again is impossible
love is just a tease
an urban legend that never happened
or at least it is for me.

So, I'll get along somehow
to keep myself preserved.
But, I'll never bloom again
until the day I leave this earth.

Heart For Sale

My heart is for sale
it is all brand new
it might not be much
but, I'll sell it to you.

If you promised to hold it
tightly with both hands
be just as careful
if you can.

And give me yours in return
I promise you're getting a good deal
I don't care if yours is used
lets see how good it can make me feel.

There's a chance I'll shy away
have a feeling I will
but, affection takes some getting used to
forgive me if my nerves can't stand still.

I have a broken heart anyway
from not trying love at all
please don't make me regret
it took so much time to want this.

I hear of all the risk
once upon a time
I felt relieved I was safe
but, the grass was greener than mine.

I have a good heart
but, it wants a home
I want to feel passion
instead of feeling alone.

I want to go off the market
lets see how the cards fold
and if I find that you understand
then, it will be sold.

Not The Same Person

Now that your back in town
I guess you looked me up
because it was you're voice on my machine
saying you're still in love.

It's been some time since you broke my heart
but, you said you were confused
now that everything died down
I have to admit to you:

I'm not the same person
that once was by your side
I've had time to grow and change
now, my mind is open wide.

There was a time I looked in your face
and couldn't tell the difference between truths or lies
I am no longer that naïve
or weak enough to cry.

I developed into this woman
you can't hurt any more
the opposite of who loved you
I am now so much more.

If you want to know this woman
that is all brand new
maybe we can have a chance
I could know the new you.

A brand new couple
exploring all the what if's
you may well have changed
after all, I did.

The Kingdom

I am the underdog
in a lion's kingdom.
Not they're friend, I am their prey
they pace at night, I see them.

Their eyes are like fire
staring into different paths.
The food wanders to them
and they get chewed up fast.

I want no business with them
I am trying to live as they are
They were given sharp fangs and speed
these short legs won't get me far.

I hide behind a bush in the night
luckily it's dark
and I hoped they wouldn't hear
the beats of my heart.

I wish we could be friends
I was branded their enemy
and once our paths cross
it will be absolute castastrophe.

I beg for an alliance
they want to wage a war
it's all about the top
it was the kingdom's lore.

But, it's the Lord's kingdom
divided into parts
but, not to be claimed as yours
to be claimed as ours.

Now, I'm not much of a contender
but, I'll work with what I have
I'll kill you with kindness
maybe you won't be so mad.

I see that fire in your eyes
my eyes extinguished long ago
but you and I combined
this kingdom becomes our world.

Dancing

Get up and dance with me
lets dance the night away
There's a little girl inside
that wants to come and play.

I am not a dancer
never had the urge before
but, somethings coming over me
the peer is our dance floor.

Dancing with you became my dream tonight
two shadows on the ground
just slow dancing in circles
letting loose when no ones around.

This is very soothing
to allow myself to move so gracefully
the waves of the ocean, silent music
lightly tapping our feet.

The stars above, our spotlight
and we wished on them all
I'm sick of standing still
sick of being afraid I'd fall.

Outside of the little girl
a women wants to come out and play
who's sick of closing up
and of being in the shade.

Never let the stars fade out
may they shine above
let us dance the night away
with our dance of love.

MELODY STARR

A Fool

They say I was his fool
and maybe I was
My trust came so easy
because I wanted to love.

They say "I told you so."
but, I don't want to hear
I'll probably do it over again
if he were here.

But, if he were to look at you
in the same way he did me
it would make you want to be
a bigger fool than me.

So, just save all your words
I know what you would do
when he would put his arms around you
you'd play a fool too.

He just has a way
of weakening the strong
of making you laugh and cry
and then saying so long.

If you were me, I know just what you would say
you wouldn't talk very well
your words would be as silly as mine
you'd buy the words he had to sell.

If you looked into his handsome face
you wouldn't see any pain
you'd be just like me
and give yourself away.

That was foolish of me
but, you'd have to be there
so, calling me a fool
wouldn't be fair.

Just leave me alone
being a fool was a small price to pay
dust myself off again
you'll understand someday.

A Date With Misery

I had a collision with misery
didn't see it coming
I would have headed for the hills
and just kept on running.

It seemed to be nowhere in sight
I guess it snuck up on me
but, it felt like a crash
by the way it hit me.

I knew it still would be around
just waiting for the right time
when it was going and a lonely day came
and I stated to feel the signs.

But, I thought i'd just think good things
and it would never find me
but, misery intruded my hiding place
it was right behind me.

I didn't want to let it in
but, it barged through the door
I really couldn't help it
and my tears begun to pour.

I tried to think of what could be
misery might not be here the next day
but, I was all alone and it didn't look so good
happiness was so far away.

There was no way to prepare
but, I know I will survive
I'll give it all I have
it's just a part of life.

The Angel Inside Of Us

I heard an angel wisper to me.
Although I couldn't see her.
I listened carefully in silence
because I was eager.

To hear what an angel has to say
to just little old me.
It must be awfully important
It felt like a dream.

She said to focus on good things
and I will live in peace
to do things that I enjoy to do
and the sadness will release.

To not let the past disappear
because it is a part of you
but, she didn't say it just to me
or even a precious few.

She will tell those who listen
and believe her to be real
there is an angel inside of us
that most don't even feel.

It's easy to forget
the goodness in our lives
until a little voice reminds us
so, don't let that voice die.

Let it ring loud and clear
and sing with you through life
we must never let go
of the angel inside.

Baggage

Everyone has their baggage to lug
bags are packed, time to move on
but, they're always moving with you
there for you to trip on.

It seems that I trip a lot
took some nasty spills
lied for a while spiritless
while others have cheap thrills.

we also carry smiles
lets see who fronts the best
or maybe I won
no contest.

Maybe I do better than I thought
everybody's a reflection on you
tears haven't fallen, still lugging them around
maybe I'm busy keeping an eye on you.

everyday we walk our own paths
and wisper our own songs
very silently we cry, carrying on
never asking what's wrong.

Two Different Men

So shifty and devious he was
with his secrets and betrayals
behind curtains where I didn't know him
there are many tall tales.

the ones I would never believe
not even by someone I trust
than, one day he wasn't expecting me
uncovered sins of control, evil and lust.

You couldn't keep secrets forever
our love faded with the man I thought I knew
you dared to show remorse
made me sorry I loved you.

I thought I had you figured out
but, there was still much to know
there's something in your eyes I couldn't see
and you will take the toll.

A different man lived in you
I didn't even see it
convincing, but not that good
to keep hiding your dirty little secrets.

Got caught in your own web
your freezing heart is tied
who knew you could be two people?
but, one of them died.

Capture

Shades of pink, orange and lavender
mixed up to make the sky.
I feel like I can almost touch it
days just keep flying by.

I can never catch the days
the most I can do is chase
to the end of the land
watch it continue as I approach water.

Or maybe I'll just take a dive
because I don't want to kiss it goodbye
it can only go on for so long
maybe I'll catch the night.

Wrapped in blue like sapphires
only much more valuable than gems
but, we never sit and admire it
for what it is.

The shooting stars go by so fast
wherever the breeze does end up
nothing can stop it
I'm in love.

I feel it in my toes
I feel it run through my hair
beams of light, beams of darkness
I'll see you tomorrow.

I like you more than I lead on
your holiness is breath taking
and if I take my last deep breathe
I'll still see you tomorrow.

Neck Of The Woods

Oh, my neck of the woods!
I love you more than I should
you kept me out of plague
but, I just can't stay here all day.

Before I get all that attached
going to see if I can find my match
out there where the sun shines
where dreams become real life.

This is my place, but I have to try
this doesn't mean goodbye
but, there are other things
people aren't as bad as they seem.

Oh my neck of the woods!
you can do some harm and some good.
You are all I know
but, things have to change.

I'll be back, it won't be long
before I feel the need to be alone
your walls will still be here for me
when I need your cover and peace.

Ireland Greens

Pick a flower in Ireland for me
in a field, colors of green
smells so lovely. holding it in my hand.
I'm in this beautiful serene land.

I have never been here before
just admiring three and four leaf clovers
on the other side of the shore
I wanted to be there more and more.

There is something in the air
that causes me to not have a care
my red hair flowing through the breeze
feeling this place travel through me.

Now I know what my ancestor's meant
this is more than I've ever dreamt
please keep me here as long as you can
where the air is fresh and I have friends.

Give me the best of luck
anywhere else, I'm always stuck
let me run in your green fields
like I'm not in a dream, but real.

Random Life

She smoked one cigarette after another
trying to get to her destination
one foot in front of the other
a part of this nation.

He, and his mo hawk and chains
very few know his name
just his eccentric sight
tidy hair and a suit, he would be the same.

Oh nation, let us be!
a little free, a little crazy
without this, would we survive
twists and turns of random life?

A little girl with her mom
eating sweet gum drops
not a care she has
in her hands, she has a lot.

A business women in heels
waiting for the cough drops to kick in
she has a presentation to give
she's going to make them spin.

Oh nation, let us be!
a little psychotic, a little angry
let us be what we were meant to be!
Oh nation, you will see.

We were chosen to be here
to make our destiny
the world's not going down the drain
Oh nation, let us be!

In Tune

This elderly lady with heart and soul
had a gift for a long time
whenever she sits at her piano bench
her heart sings every line.

A genius lies in her
she often does not set free
when she plays, she's truly happy
and it comes out in the keys.

Once a child taking lessons
she goes in the present days
she has aged, her heart and soul are young
like a girl again at play.

She never stopped playing in her dreams
she plays for others and herself
such energy, such grace
the music is deeply felt.

In every heart there is talent
that never really dies
it's repetition after death
in memories combined.

Peculiar

She wakes up with her shoes on
just crashing on the couch
her heart is full of dreams
her head is full of doubt.

Walking around the neighborhood
in her pajamas and bare feet
nobody ever see's her cry
out and about in the street.

She is a peculiar girls indeed
talking with sharp words
that never pierce anybody
but she bites her tongue sometimes.

Everyone see's her scream
run wild with a smile
she's falling down the stairs
she walks her talk.

They like having her around
she's funny in a lot of ways
she makes life interesting
she's quite a case.

My Heart Will Not Die

My heart will not die
because of a heartless man
it won't sink to the bottom of the ocean
or get buried in the sand.

It was in perfect beat before we met
and it still can be
you are not the reason I have it
it loves me.

It has plenty more to do
It won't turn black because of you
I learned a lesson by accident
have people around me to get through.

It has all the love I need
inside of it and more
when I have it for someone else or not
it will go on even if it has a sore.

I will not spend the day
under the covers wishing everything away
I won't spend the nights
crying into a pillow until it gets light.

My heart lives, it's not through
nor will it turn bitter
it will make due
I'm not a quitter.

Me Beyond

What do they see under the sugary pines
under the sweetness and light?
beneath what doesn't matter
beyond the tongue I bite?

I don't just lay it out there mostly
whats to become of me?
the anger, sadness and hatred of people
the person I can't be.

What if you don't accept all of me?
was I even meant to walk this planet?
all this anxiety I'm sure everyone has
so why can't I stand it?

never know what to say in a crowd
I'm a different kind of lady
don't mind me can you leave
I'm just damn crazy.

so, I guess I'll come out
and let them deal
they can leave if they want
if I'm too real.

And if they stay, they always will
friends side by side
they will see I am good
I must try

In Hate With You

I hated you before I loved you
y never grew on me
didn't know what I was getting into
barking up the wrong tree.

Once my eyes saw the candy
I forgot everything else
nothing sweet in my life
you've made it a living hell.

Get a last minute phone call from a friend
you cancelled our plans
heaven forbid I ever did the same
you want me at your command.

Mysteriously disappear to God knows where
ignore me when you're not alone
spend most of the time on he phone
tell me to be quiet in a loud tone.

If I knew what I know now
if I ever see you it'd be too soon
plenty of fish in the sea
saying goodbye to you.

This is a lesson I'll take with me
in the future it'll help me too
need to find someone to enjoy
I'm so in hate with you.

In Writing

These are the words written on my soul
which never wash out
staying there without a smudge
the lines I want to shout.

When I close my book
the feelings linger in my spirit
they are oh so real
can you feel it?

Everything I am and am not
piecing myself together
me spelled out in magic
to you, my heartfelt letters.

They are my footprints, my fingerprints
my destiny and intensity
my soul dug out
please say you believe.

So overwhelming
makes me laugh, smile and bleed
taking this all in
please say "you touched me."

And if more books spill out of me
I'm sure they will knowing me
be there some steps of the way
and say that you believe.

The Last Kiss

Please give me a kiss good bye
before forever without you starts
won't make much difference but it's important now
while I still have your heart.

I want to know your last kiss is coming
so I can take a beath
give me all of you through your lips
lets not hold back, take it to our death.

Please give me a hug and wish me well
lets end it like that
our lives and love were too short
so I'll let you walk your path.

Lets enjoy out company a while more
start in opposite directions when the sun comes up
it won't be that easy for me
but, for the last time, I want to feel your touch.

And ride the memories home
drop off lessons in our minds
keep our hearts open
I want to enjoy our last time.

Sending You

I'll send you a bleeding kiss
right smack on the lips
these lips know pain
and they reminisce.

I'll send you a wink in my eye
through the clouds in the autumn sky
send you these things one at a time
because I can't all at once make you mine.

Fragments of my thoughts
like expensive wine
gulp it all up
you ran out of time.

Like it like this, full of surprise
enjoy, I'm unfolding
patience for your prize
come get me.

Send me back what I gave
we both need to be saved
and on one enchanting day
I'll still be sending you.

Extension

The sun revives me at six a.m.
the sky is amazing and unusual
if I had wings, it would still be too breathtaking to reach
all these colors, it's neverending.

If the planet were a battlefield
fighter's at sunrise
take a look at this ball of peace
and open up your eyes.

Earth becomes sensual
the sky seduces me
the air's erotic, my skin is thin
I was dead before it brought on my sensibilitity.

My thoughts are only on this
I give you my full attention
no distractions, separate from you
you give my life extenstion.

Rise Above

I rise above
the dark frosty sky
I do this as much as I can
especially times I cry.

I rise above
my ears are ringing
the symphony's playing
and it's time to start singing.

I am lonely in this place
in many places
in all places I get scared
of all these faces.

But, I rise again
I get past
all anger and despair inside
so I can last.

I rise above
feeling dead
life's fast paced
only inside my head.

I rise some more
when on solid ground
trying to find strength inside
I get so down.

I rise above
the beauty never changes
I till find luck
in random paces.

Hope lives on
just a smile away
I rise above
an aweful place.

Tire Tracks

She sped off in another direction
in her car, to the highway
she's in a hurry to change her life
too many days like yesterday.

Her eyes are on the road
she's wiping the slate clean
thinking of how things are going to be different
she had to cut some strings.

People are waving her goodbye
but, there's a chance she will be back
if she can be what she is there, here
she will follow the tire tracks.

Living for herself
how long has it been?
lifting the weights off her soul
to see what else is within.

needs to realize she is important
and put her first for a chance
build herself up again
so she won't come tumbling down.

Spirit Of Immortality

A free spirit in love with the wind
soared above many trees
and when you can hear leaves move
you'll know it's me.

Spirits of the ground: it's been so long
but, it's only for the time being
I can't come down to visit you
but through the air, always hear me singing.

I can see you but, you can't see me
it's just part of the rules
you look so beautiful at this view
but, I can't fly down to touch you.

I don't know how long it will be
before your immortality
I'll be waiting for your presence
though it's now, I want you flying up to me.

Patience the hardest part of it
but, I feel our souls combine
sometimes you feel so near to me but
you have to escape because you're not just mine.

I've swam in the shy day and night
and you really must try it
I'll really try to stop wanting you so much
and adore you and be quiet.

Mother's Songs

Mother, will you sing to me
like the good old days?
I'd really like to be there again
your voice still so beautiful today.

You may pick any song you'd like
I'm so fond of them all
they've always made everything right
every since I could crawl.

Pease let there be more golden days of song
as I lie in bed and look up at you
feel peace and love travel through thick walls
and I truly love you.

I am fully grown now
but, I yearn to hear
the songs you made lovely
sung into my ear.

I couldn't forget you
you and song gave me life
I can make it on my own
but, will you sing to me tonight?

you love to sing, I can tell
by tell by the look in your eye
it's been long, I've missed it
will you sing to me tonight?

MELODY STARR

In Your Hands

Keeper of my soul, hold on tight
think it's going to be a rough night
don't want to lose when I have little
so I'm writing you a riddle.

I know only you could understrand
how I appreciate what you hold in your hand
you are that one special person
who holds me together, behind the curtain.

I see your eyes when looking at stars
now I know you're not so far
from me and my trouble life
and believe me, you are a sight!

Whenever I decide to dust my heart
you are there to give it a spark
falling asleep from my thoughts
you will never let my soul; be lost.

When God shines down on me
the cosmos never looked so lovely
the day you give my soul back
I'll probably put it on my lap.

Which is why it is for you to keep
have a part of me that you can't beat
soul keeper, if you're job ever gets done
I'll get to see you one on one.

Splendor

Your amazing I any light
in the dark, you still have an earth shattering presence
I'm absolutely fond of you
without question.

There is no agony or torture
just don't leave my side
your love is abundance
and I need it even after I die.

Anybody would be proud to know you
in the twilight I am next to you
my heart is around your finger
yours is around mine too.

I appreciate you so
love in all it's splendor
still can't believe what's in front of me
until you touch me.

The Funeral

I stood by his side in silence
battling what to say or do
there are no winners in words or action
when his father's life is through.

The day he wished would never happen
the funeral home is still and cold
I don't know if I should stay silent
the words by others got old.

Nothing can make it better
I love him, so I cried too
seeing him this way is so painful
saying goodbye to a man I never really knew.

According to him, his father broke the mold
he wanted his girlfriend there for him
but, I don't know how to play the role
and he's just holding it in.

After the service it was him and i
I grabbed him and held tight
he clinged to me and thanked me
for being with him tonight.

I told him I hope he knew
life had a lot in store for him
even though a long road laid out ahead
his father was in the wind.

Said I was sorry for not
knowing what to do
he said it was comforting with me
and we turned in until the sun came through.

Being Alright

She's insane. Your wildest dream
she doesn't see what you see
you see the glass as half full
she see's it completely empty.

Everything that comes her way
is damned, not even explained
through all this
she remains tame.

She can love in any way
but, her heart is bleeding excessively
but, just a few tears come out
and she's on to the next thing.

She has the power to impress you
she has the strength inside
she may be wrapped in pain
but, she's going to be alright.

Nobody is worrying
she will land right in place
she has trouble reading people
like reading a blank face.

She never knows what she's getting into
until she's neck deep
she digs herself out
like it never happened.

She loves herself deep down
gets through the day fine
everyone's glad to know her
she's going to be alright.

Recklessly In Love

Love me recklessly
don't let me back away
from your love and your good intensions
let me stay.

Let me stay in this bliss
stranded for miles
far away from fear
only in our style.

Let reckless be our way
to love as no one has
those who are too careful
end up with a relationship gone bad.

Leave me guessing
of what we will do next
love me bravely
better than the rest.

Recklessly fall in love
so deep I'll always have you
and let them watch and wish the same
and I'll recklessly love you.

Never thought I'd be reckless with my heart
but with you, it feels right
love me recklessly
more each day and night.

Creeping Around Your Heart

I creep around your heart
try to sneak my way in
doing all the big and little things
so you will let me in.

It took time to find it
your hiding behind a blank face
but, I did that's half the battle
and it's not such a dark place.

Try to make you laugh
walk on my tip toes
I never caught you off guard
it's not over though.

I'll creep around your heart
randomly, here and there
and you won't always be watching
I'll win on a dare.

You'll thank me later
I almost have the combination
to the heart hurt and afraid
slowly, with concentration.

I'll make it better
it won't be so dark
I'll get you soon
I creep around your heart.

Falling

You have a lot of layers to go through
if my eyes re the key to my soul
I see you searching endlessly
I start to lose control.

Just as another strong layer forms
it just as easily falls
your eyes are burning through me
I hope your not a fraud.

I try to slip steadily
but I come tumbling down
I'm not made of concrete
your eyes always catch me.

Heart, soul, and flesh
can all still be mine
don't take it all away from me
and everything will be fine.

Spilling my guts to you
I see you searching endlessly
there's still a lot of me left

Anyone At All

The golden gates of behaviour
the pride a brick wall
the mystic of the girl
who could be anyone at all.

Closed shades in the darkness
the open book continues speaking
pages and pages of the unknown
always repeating.

Look in the women's eyes
tell what you do know
she intrigues you I hope
loves from her toes.

You want to solve this puzzle
countless layers of her soul
hidden in expressions of mutiny
but sin free with no foes.

But, you will know the essentials
and possibly things in between
when she gives clues to her being
she'll disappear like a dream.

Mysterious lady
what's behind those eyes?
behind that smile?
were dying to know why!

Why are you as broad as the horizon?
are you meant to be
as unlimited as the sky
with flashes of lightening?

Walking with your heels clicking
but your tongue bit and soundless
creeping around corners
yet, surrounding us.

More than a lifetime to know
grapping your every characteristic
with a sweetheart smile
you also see mischief.

The golden gates of behavior
the pride, a brick wall
the mystic of the girl
who could be anyone at all.

Late Nighters

The warriors come out with their swords
as soon as the night hits the sky
when it's dark and anything can happen
the sun says it's goodbye.

Before the cheery light in the morning
the night begins and ends
brings out the animals
and anything else it can.

Making it's bold statement
stars regard the earth
late nighter's celebrate
before the daybreaker's emerge.

Fireplaces and covers
a midnight walk
how ever you spend your evening
before the sun talks.

Gazing into the eyes of another
or spending it all alone
some want to see the night go
some don't.

But another will come
just like the days
the earth revolves again
for the daybreaker's and late nighter's.

What She Is

She is light wrapped in darkness
shimmering behind the dusk
and on any or all occasions
you'll find yourself in love.

In her arms is where you'll want to be
or sometimes as far as far as possible
because she gathers up the leaves
a brush of wind will come.

Making her start all over on you
you'll never know who she is
secrets in her eyes never tell
but, what a beautiful person she gives.

She really pulls it off
keeps it together when she needs to
she's too good to be true but she is
and you don't have a clue.

Because she'll keep you guessing
she will draw you in
take your heart before you knew what happened
a legend as long as she lives.

Songbird

Songbird sing me a new song
until the sun is gone
songbird what will you sing today
in your beautiful colors chirping away?

Songbird, will you sing a song for me
way up in your tree?
give me the little things in life
and I will be on my way.

Musical bird, show me the rhythum of the day
harmonious expressions make me stay
early risers love to sing
nature is speaking.

Songbird, fly away
this is the end of the day
the night has to make it's appearance
but, there will be another concert.

Halo

When the halos off I wonder
if the devil will pull me under
How could I want to be so dark
when I have the purest heart?

Take me to the dungeon
I am the last sacrifice
you look with red eyes
then I want to get back to life.

My good deeds are left undone
I have more work to do
sometimes I'm not happy
but I am miserable with you.

Low self esteem talked
now it has nothing to say
I will be on the Lord's side
your losing me today.

There's too few of me
I will be happy with who I am
I won't let occasional bad times
make me a part of your land.

When the halo was off
and given a far toss
it was always standing by
not so deep inside.

I will always find it
I knew I was in a place I didn't belong.

Compulsive

Loving him is so compulsive
I beg God for strength
because I don't want to be like this
I've stayed with him at great lengths.

I smile half the time he's around
he sure knows how to put me down
he's the king of my misery and heart
for both, he wears the crown.

Never knew by saying those three words
could keep me in such a bad situation
but when he says them I've never been so happy
thank God he doesn't leave me.

God, make me stronger
don't know if I can take anymore
don't know if I can live without him
but, what am I with him for?

Imagining life without him, I fall to the floor
in relief and heartache.

Subtle

Love: open my mind once again
to a sugar land where tree tops are high
and always soothing, always blooming
with you I aim for he sky.

He makes me see in a different light
no dimness, not blinding, but full blown
the temperature rises comfortably
he has courage to do what I won't.

My love doesn't give me too much
that's not what love is
my expectations aren't high or low
just want to be his miss.

He doesn't have to over do it
to make me feel such a way
I fell deep and want to go back
my itinerary is his everyday.

I have found the deepest joy
got straight to the soul of him
if only all felt like this, didn't change minds
their light wouldn't be so dim.

Bad Night's Sleep

The merit isn't so bright in most eyes
I give you all my devotion
I keep my end of the bargains
I gave it all until I bled.

Virtue doesn't always win
it gets you good nights sleep
can't let my sugary side
absorb the rest of me.

You were blinded by my twilight
but didn't pay me any mind
took my generosity
and butted me in line.

Some nights i'd rather toss and turn
with pounding in my head
and laugh at the hell I've raised
and evil words I've said.

I was a fallen angel
with her eyes on the flame
landed in an ocean where it could do no harm
maintained a good name.

The greenest of the grass
looked lonely and washed out
I am the same person, just curious
of what the other side was about.

Without goodness, don't know who I'd be
irrational thoughts of sin
mind wandering to red
won't change who I am within.

Maintain my good name even in bad times
I stay on this side
where it is most natural
and undeniable I still have my wings.

A Toast

Me and this man drank a toast
in the moonlit peace before us
to a hundred lonely nights that are over
and evolved into complete trust.

We kept picking up broken pieces
to get where we are now
we laughed at careless lovers
who didn't have the know how.

We knew this day would come
so much, better than our dreams
like a delirious haze but real
we make a great team.

Decit has no place here
not afraid to get carried away
I'm laughing and clinging to your arms
it was worth the decay.

a love like this was never known to me
and now I'm going to boast
I'm inspired and free spirited
as we make our next toast.

Uncover

I've hugged and kissed everyone goodbye
closed the door to the outside
my brain spinning with ideas
you wouldn't dare come inside.

No intention of harm
something so powerful inside of me
innocence stays through the middle of the night
but, somewhere dawn doesn't want to be.

Smokes coming from underneath the door
my form is groundbreaking
I'm growing as a person so much
like quick sand the floor is caving.

I'm not saying goodbye to who I used to be
it's all under control
my charm becomes spellcasting
with brewing potions I don't even know.

Catching the wind in my hand
I know i's nonsense to you
my hair is flowing
can't wait to share this with you.

I know I can
with everything in me
all good depth lives here
come in and see.

Blind Folded

The moon blindfolds the sky
very few stars lay about
the tunnels of the city are shadows
the sun has temporarily moved out.

My picnic blanket is drenched with rain
the heels of my shoes are slipping home
everyone has scattered inside
but, I'm outside all alone.

It was a good day I suppose
I think under the moonlight
the heavens will allow the sun back again
I have dark circles from a sleepless night.

More friends to chase tomorrow
more life to lead
how many sidewalks will I walk across
before it's the sun that I will see?

The sun doesn't always guarantee a good day
we will just have to wait and see.

Intense

Emotionally exhausted
throwing the pen across the desk
get up and click away in my heels
another poem is sent.

I rung myself out like a sponge
until I was dry and couldn't feel
I've reread and felt them over again
I am truly revealed.

I've put in so much but it came so easy
I sat back sweating and crying
my guts wrenched to the page
but inside I am now smiling.

I've made it into art
I've done something with this
something deep, intense and beautiful
you can't turn away from it.

Found somewhere I fit
where I don't struggle with words

Until the next unloading
I will take a breath
learning more about myself
you won't know what I'm thinking next.

Involved

The heat generates from my body
as I take in the goods
from the earth feeling the soft soil
on my bare foot.

Good nature is my reward
and my love is here to give
the grains of my soul are growing healthy
as I continue to live.

I am involved in all things
I invite you to this day
to the sound of my voice
hear the words I have to say.

We are not irreparable
you turned into something I can't fight anymore
all the words come cross my mind
and I don't know what's in store.

I will not stand as a statue
rough with a steel grin
I'll have my heart in your company
my strength comes from within.

Combat

Didn't bring a shield to this fight
just all of my flesh and bone
not weighing myself down with all the rest
life is waiting for me to come home.

I have to face you first
my ego is already hurt
you can't do much to the rest of me
the best of me is too deep.

You can't touch just my skin
I'll bear my wounds with a grin
all your seduction won't matter
I'll overcome it all.

Fighting words is what you do most
I'm even ready for cutthroat
Being underestimated is my advantage
Overrated is what you manage.

Come for you again
when I break free
from your weak grip
that you loosened expectedly.

I subsist taken in more nourishment
when this melee ends
this experience will be lesson
and I could possibly gain a friend.

Living Ghost

If you don't believe in living ghost
you think it's a fallacy
all you have to do
is take a look at me

A clouded figure
see through, feet not touching the ground
hiding in day, lurking at night
you don't hear a sound.

Leading a silent life
knocking things down
but, all you see is an open window
I'm white and chain bound.

I don't even get to haunt
i's the living earth that's haunting me
you've walked through me plenty
I haven't arrived and I can't leave.

Stuck in between life and death
neither seem to be inviting

I am not supernatural, I am real
I wish you could see
I'm one lonely living ghost
with no one to summon me.

Declaration

Look through my eyes
let me show you all my passion
every time pen and paper call my name
nobody else can do it in my fashion.

I can never tell enough it seems
my demeanour becomes irrelevant
I'll use my freedom to express
when my voice isn't telling it.

I am devoted to my gift
it can be as powerful as I
it will reach down and grab the pit of your stomach
until the day I die.

I feel very strongly
as these words surround me
Which one will I reach for today
to get through this audience?

Feelings haunt my heart
words overrun my mind
they will not be buried or laid to rest
they take turns through time.

And I am lucky enough
to have a way to declare
and have them there
so the rest of me won't tear.

Back And Forth

Cupid I wish I had a choice
but my heart is at war
as usual with no victory to reach
and I keep going back and forth.

I'm fragile, shall I not love?
careless hearts are out of their cages
but never hungry for mine
even when my vulnerable hand raises.

Heart loving and fresh beyond compare
so, why would no man ever dare
or even be aware?
like I have a sign that says "beware."

Is my heart ready
for something I've dreamed
since I was a teen?
love continues to tease.

Cupid, would it not be right?
Is that why I'm kept lonely
night after night?
Am I stuck with me?

Being the center of someone's life
just give it a try
maybe I'll do right
when no one else abides.

Cupid: make up my mind for me.

Lovesick

He was just a vision
and I was only a visitor
until he stood all too real
I'm existing as a prisoner.

But, I am not lovesick
not when I saw him unarrayed
I'm just sick of love
he stood for nothing I could take.

This homeless heart let him in
not he's only a reminder
he tried to sew it up with I'm sorry
he couldn't be blinder.

I'm banishing love from me
I'd rather my heart live in the streets
just pumping blood, no feelings
platonic with everyone I meet.

Something I never really thought about
made me so bitter
the thread is breaking on my heart
and I am a admitter.

Neglect and disappointment
is just too tough
but, I am not lovesick
I'm just sick of love.

Cash

Money burns
as we run through it
wallets get thin
and our pockets too.

Lets see how fast it goes
every week
things we want
and what we need.

Excessive spending
barely making it
fresh new bills
make the most of it.

Hunger for more
it can make us smile
we have to spend
and occasionally run wild.

Living poorly
or living in style
we've alive
enjoy it a while.

Living large
for the cash
don't worry so much
but, it just goes too fast.

Wide Open

A place of soothing therapy
my hearts secrets
capture powerful words
mean every word of it.

Supplying more mystery
with a harsh tongue
you didn't think was mine
until me and my pen became one.

When everybody tries to label me
and I pretend to go along
I will have a chance to be heard
there is somewhere I do belong.

you can't treat it as nonsense
I'll shut you down
it will leave a presence in you
that won't always be found.

It cuts me wide open
I deny no more
look it in the eyes, take it in
accept all parts of myself.

From The Ground Up

The tallest tree survived
the sky is a woman of change
smell the morning from the ground up
night murdered without pain.

Born again tomorrow
with a different view
as it is needed
the old one will be no use.

Difference may be subtle
but it is there
something new wakes or sleeps
freshens the air.

Open us wide
sweet toned or dead
never see anything melt
this flower is kept.

My Darkness

The sun visits me briefly
I cry out for it's return
it doesn't
it's decision was firm.

Keep my eyes open
as wide as I can
no longer have a shadow
darkness is my shadow.

It has a never ending attraction
drawn to me
gripping to my bones
how faithful can it be?

It's like nothing else
a huge part
it holds me in comfort
understands my dark heart.

I am not lonely after all
I did get something
how shallow am I?
I'll continue lugging.

Learn things I need to learn
un focus a good time
don't have to dream simple anymore
when the sun returns I won't be so blind.

Heard

Your presence seals me tight
I can't breathe
locked down inside
trapped words echo in me.

Never to see the pit
I'm bottomless
words are feeding on the bottom of the floor
my savor and annoyance is quietness.

Accept your words
which run to the end of time
never clear my throat
I just choke on mine.

My lips sewed with stiches
taunt my personality
as your lips flap on and on
they are as tireless as me trying to speak.

I run out of subjects quickly
Do you think I'm listening to you?
Do we listen to each other?
nodded head are no proof.

Used words are just the same
I will never speak like this
you got me talking in my sleep
with words I didn't get to use.

No one or thing gets in my way now
this is how I use my words
maybe your listening now
I'm being heard.

Back

Forced to single status again
no anticipation for the next love
stubbornness drilled into my brain
my heart was stuffy and ad enough.

I shrug my shoulders in defeat
that is what you want of me
an you had it for while
until I reclaimed my style.
Reclining was too easy
I recite y power
I'm back and ready to win
and 'll say it louder.

My heart is skillful
I won't let it go to waste
little more prepared this time
and I say who I face.

When it's not a competition anymore
and we become a team
my precious love will be yours
with all of my being.

And, again if things don't go that way
I'll desend to where I need to, but resurface
the prize can be mine
not a copy, and I'll deserve it.

Love Drunk

I'm coming down
I'm not love drunk anymore
my head spun for you
now, I am just sore.

Not smiling idiotically
by just being happy to have you
I have that feeling in my stomach
but the hangover is through.

The tiny sips you fed me
clouded the rest
it never felt real
mediocure at best.

I felt no strength
but I leaped to your love
like a skiddish child who
didn't know what to dream of.

Didn't know what was ahead
didn't wait it out
my feet stumbled to you
but, you didn't have the know how.

I'm under the influence of me now
gotten over being drowsy
awake and I know where to begin
love drunk, I leave.

These Days

Pen in my hand ready to go!
whenever there's something
wrong with the world's flow.

Or is it mine
that seems so confined?
these thoughts need to resign.

Tommorow is going to happen, like it or no
doesn't need me, I need it
nothing on me fits.

Dreams skyrockets out of my hands
and all seems lost
it what I've come across.

Outer space in my head
just a place for me to have
when I feel off the map.

Precious lies keep me going
all sin keeps prevoking
expression I continue evoking.

I summon my inner soul
dark corners so unknown
world, get a taste of my tongue.

Every time I turn around
my feet are spilling off the ground
some times I feel like God's clown.

Then, my pen is to the page
where i can talk with grace
thank God for these days.

Young

A little girl walking down the street
chewing bubble gum
eyes on her feet.

Youth barricaded by rules
a life to choose
unknown of the blues.

Barouque curls around her face
no cares, all make believe
adulthood, she tries to escape.

Muddy shirt and all
loud and full of questions
beautiful not to mention.

Barely able to view past the fence
hardly a couple feet from the ground
no scars and no dents.

All hurt wiped away
by a kiss
and automatically brave.

Before we had to be smart
or know what we know now
in youth we didn't care, we were proud.

A Rebuilding

Throw ordinary living out the window
drink the seas
seldom come up for air
please join me.

On fresh ground, fresh eyes
don't live as if liveless
creativity is beautiful
imagination is priceless.

Don't let this only work for a day
let it pour from you as a waterfall
quenched more day by day
be unique after all.

Supply yourself with all you need
no such thing as overestimating
surprise yourself in amazement
come on, I'm waiting.

Blocked

It's maddening to a writer
to be at a loss for words
even if it's temporary
the emotions stir.

The minutes soar as I sit here
so passionate to write and
ideas aren't rising to the occasion
words are unplanned.

I'm inflamed at this mind
drawing a blank
can't get enough and there's never too much
don't have enough length.

Usually jot down with excitement
that all this is coming from me
my pen is lazy tonight
need to express something.

But, I am a barricaded writer tonight
spoiled I suppose somewhere down the line
the words always flow so quickly
but, I will retire for the night.

I am always a writer
even when my pen is not
see what words a later time will bring
while I am stuck in this spot.

On The Loose

I'm on the loose
no leash or collar
coming at all directions
owning a mere dollar.

And I'm running
my feet can't be still
I'm free and taking advantage
there's time to fill.

I am not breathless
I breath my life
sit back for the night
and enjoy all that's in my sight.

Not running away from anywhere
once in a while, I stop and stare
my heart's rising to something new
I'm entering if I dare.

Let Us Get Acquainted

Let us get acquainted, Mother Earth
a thousand seasons have passed
since I granted you it seems
I remember how you made me laugh.

The wind teases me
I hear it hitting the window's glass
I want to become a part of it
but get held back.

Of all doubts that shouldn't be
and silence imprisons me
it likes me lonely
every day it tells me.

But, those time are becoming long gone
never thought I'd be that strong
or feel I do belong
all my life long.

I built myself up to a good place
and my lips raise upon my face
I get higher day by day
and have much more to say.

I thought you didn't want to hear
paranoia held hands with fear
my time is near
took a long time to get here.

Not letting a part of myself go
it does know me very well
but, outside parties will help
I also have secrets to tell.

I'll walk all the corners
and finally be at ease
I know you are waiting for me
but, you will always be with me.

Emotional Waves

Don't need you to feed me words
thank you, I have my own
they may be hidden in my smokey outer layers
they come out in time.

Just when my thoughts are organized
the wrench is thrown
a complete mess is made in me
and I don't know which feeling to own.

They all call my name at once
and tug at my heart
cold and warm hands try to get in
emotions stop and start.

I am only one person
Can I feel all this at once?
a hat has dropped, a feeling escaped
for that empty spot, here comes another one.

Guess I have to ride these emotional waves
until they decide to call it a day
scream to God to bring them on
so I can write more days.

So, don't need you to feed me a personality
I have enough here
get overwhelmed as much as possible
and smile at a tear.

MELODY STARR

My Detective Eyes

I see with my detective eyes
you act so inconspicuous
that in fact, it should be criminal
because you must know this.

You attract me in many ways
your triumphant in love
your up for my traditions
you love me just enough.

I was just a pedestrian
no thumb in the sky
I was no model passenger
until I saw with my detective eyes.

The man that wasn't hiding
no crime to commit
I was the one who was puzzled
this is the one your with.

I have done better since
tied all ties
there was nothing wrong
with my detective eyes.

The culprit was my guard
standing way too tall
I can accept a good man
after those crimes after all.

But, you must let me say all this
or it would be a crime
your one in a million I see
with my detective eyes.

Blurry Yesterday

No questioned smiles
no feelings held back
we were children
Imagine that.

I can squint to a blurry yesterday
with the sun in my eyes
my neighbors were my friends
until they locked they're doors tight.

Everyone knew you were sad
because you shown how you felt
no embarrassment or denial
asked for help.

Before life screwed you up
you were free to roam so far
not much emotional pain
slept on the way home in your parent's car.

We seldom hold any hand now
we move ourselves out of harm's way
something's we don't see coming
but, every hurt is a lesson in a way.

Friends had all the time
responsibilities out of the way
we try to squeeze in plans
instead of just walking out to play.

Some I miss, some not so much
but once in a while I'll go back
we were children
Imagine that.

Like Nothing

The last sigh
at the days beginning and end
looking to get my fill
a lover and friend.

Then he gave my imagination a rest
like nothing I ever dreamt
excitement with my every step
and I'm never spent.

I'll never feel dead again
I live all of my days
love is as real as my emotions
I can love in so many ways.

Leave tears in yesterday
where they belong
shake them off, done me no good
wasn't crying for the others for long.

I feel reality
like an earthquake
that calms and starts again
and leaves me not to forget.

Thought I was confined
to solitare
until you took me out of there
my heart finally shared.

Sign Off

Time to match the sparkle
escaping my eyes
search all the words I know
sensilbilities never just pass me by.

I take it in and enjoy
sit back and let it go
lingering for next time
nice and slow.

If I ever reach the bottom of me
I'll just have to break ground
and shake out every drop
before I think of letting myself stay bound.

Nothing will stop me
the words surface
from my heart to my mind
I prevail encouraged.

Making sense
or just words piece by piece
it will never look
like scribble to me.

When I sign off
between me and the Lord
I smile between us
before I let others aboard.

Some feelings do hurt
but, it's almost like food
sending me inspiration
when I'm in the mood.

Night Light

Day is my enemy
until it gets dark
I'm at war as the hours drag
night is where my life starts.

It has all the day to stir up trouble
all "open" signs jump out at me
save routines for the sun
light up the streets!

Darkness can change everything
passion built up inside
personalities days have yet to see
it is here that I confide.

All light is from the moon
intriguing people to greet
I don't sense any danger
in the moonlit street.

The sun shows no mercy to my eyes
but, soon it will have it's turn
make it through the next twelve hours
until then, my patience burns.

Withheld

All these layers sew me up
in silence, shyness and feverishness
they also make me feel imprisoned
when I am alone, I am a misfit.

This skin doesn't burst
in this still remaining body
forget to clear my throat when I speak
peeling when seen by nobody.

All this character and imagination
gone to waste
as if it were terrible
but, it's my only independent place.

I am only a prisoner of myself
I must doctor my soul
others that are true will accept me
but, i'm always afraid that isn't so.

Jot down my every thought
it does little good
not all that ease in my shell
I'd tear it down if I could.

There's only one way to find out
much happier that way
be the whole person after so long
sometimes a little strength comes from a lot of pain.

The World And Me

Before I live
I have to make sense
I promised myself
my heart is restless to find out.

A boy has to save me just one dance
so many won't give me a chance
I am not a teenager anymore
but, just as wonderous.

The morals are fading
people are getting worse
they tell you they care
then leave you in the dirt.

Do they know how much that hurts?
so much ink later
still trying to figure out
how life and me could intertwine.

Hold on with all my energy
and go out kicking and screaming
and crying like a child
who can't say no to time.

Before we get too uptight
and drown in misery
before easier days arrive
join it one day at a time.

Shadow Up The Stairs

The past is my shadow
going up the stairs of life
holding on to the railings somewhat
more strength every time I survive.

Distractions at every turn
I never go straight ahead
my pillow case wet with tears
just before I get my rest.

My head never stops dreaming
My heart will ache again
I want so much to be real
love doesn't know who I am.

But, the days are going
some lessons have to bruise
so there can be winners
a lot will have to lose.

People won't always be standing by
waiting to comfort you
but, i have to speak up
so someone will have a clue.

I fell and had to start again
but, I hope it never ends
as I write my emotions with a pen
my attacker and best friend.

I'll have to search for energy
my shadow has to stay behind
but, it'll be right behind me
when I search randomly inside.

Everything I came across
I'll tuck into my skin
some things will always be there
when there's more being added to my shadow.

Anchors Away

I sail into sleep
once all that is on my mind is aside
and my eyes don't open until morning
blues and blacks across the sky.

Ridiculous dreams
red blooded serious emotions
can wait for tomorrow
concerns are frozen.

All colors of early dawn pass me
as I'm sound until one color settles
the dust of day is cleaned
with nights precious metals.

Wake with one more day's experience
twenty four hours wiser
some of the same day tasks
but, I have the inspiration of fire.

Drifting to sleep
with sounds of the city
both quiet and loud enough
imagine it pretty.

Take a sigh
stretch out our legs
the ship has come in
until anchor's away.

Enough wind to take me
there and home
the world is sailing with
I'm not on my own.

Taste Of A Kiss

Will i love the last?
Laugh the last?
all this time behind me
a semi full past.

Will all this time make it different?
Just to be kissed by a dirty tongue?
Unfolded in heat and lust
not knowing where it came from.

Tasting bitter from past his past nights
laying down the line on me
Would mine have any taste?
How hell or heaven sent can a kiss be?

What feeling would rush through me?
Would I feel cheated?
bending my knees, rolling back my eyes
follow the way he leaded?

Everybody knows, but I say "who knows?"
maybe he can make his kisses brand new
If i fell too deep in the moment
he could be just for me.

High Heels

Slipped into a steel toe
I stomped I tip toed
onto millions of floors
from the top to the sole.

I picked up my feet
I scraped the sidewalk
I discovered the streets
I stood and talked.

I clicked and clacked
my way to events
making history
with the rest.

Until i couldn't take another step
all the colors of envy in their eyes
proud to wear these heels
it works every time.

The only pair i own
they'e my favorites naturally
because they have to be
given a choice, I'd still pick these.

The path is cleared
the ground is not solid sometimes
like quick sand pulling me down one limb at a time
but, they free me just in time.

I emerge to continue
my heels are dug in
and they're still brand new
but, broken in.

The Cemetary

Fresh day at the cemetary
the soil is still wet
in between heaven and hell
a different fate they met.

The gates open and squeak
awaiting visitors
the buriel ground'rested well
restless souls stir.

The air is cold
giving off an eerie feeling
different lives, different deaths
this is a graveyard for immortal beings.

A profusion of sadness
of those who lost to another life
alot of tears cried here
some spirits want a fight.

The day gets dark
only a light here and there
all the stories the dead could tell
but, we won't be there.

It is between them
we wouldn't interfere
have respect for them
remember, one day we will be here.

Eyelids

The moon in this dark sky
closes me in a quilt
and calls me to rest
I abandon this day at it's kill.

My depleted mind stops wondering
releasing all my cares tonight
my eyelids drop until the scent of
the first morning flower that pulls me to life.

Halloween skies are vibrant
and wordless or so my eyes
barely see as my lids cover them
the trees sway gently before sunlight.

I subpoena wild dreams
the ceiling is the last thing i see
my senses need energy
that's what sleep brings to me.

In a warm I bid you goodnight
for I've inhaled the entire day
I bid you goodnight
before I bid you good day.

MELODY STARR

Betray

I liked the beat of my own drum
but somewhere, someway
I didn't move
to the music anymore.

There was no passion
to go on with the show
don't know if there's a rhythum
out there for me.

I'm the same girl
with different needs
the same girl and new girl
aren't holding hands as they should.

They're not in this together
development has been postponed
until I know
what I want.

A subtle replacement
time starts without me
the old girl refrains
and shyness steps in.

The cup is half empty
my mind and imagination
are too large
for my actions.

I'm pacing but tired
my body is exhausted
from my expectations
scarred due to failures.

They go their separate ways
and betray each other everyday
still getting carried away.

His Next Step

My hair traveling with the wind
my locks moved with rhythum
my breath is warm and steady
and my eyes are ready.

Wondering his next step
after buckets of my love splashed
all over him physically and with my eyes
I asked them not to tell me lies.

His beauty stood strong
eyes would never fall off him
we kept our private moments
in a memory we never closed.

Beams of smiles made me up
into a peaceful happy soul
surrounding a spirit that wanted more
but, our feelings are controlled.

Picture love however you want
thrill never leaves me
he would never let that happen
he is what I need him to be.

Eavesdropper

A fight down the street
someone packing their bags
my eyes and ears are busy
with clean hands.

Watching trouble
emerge from basements
every open window
an invitation.

They don't even know I am here
but, I know what's going on
I don't mean to be nosy
but, you wouldn't believe what my ears fell upon.

Lives are a show
until the sun falls
news develops
prelude curtain calls.

People are too loud
needing an audience
blowing preportions out
activating my glance.

I do this just once in a while
makes life intriguing
to hear others troubles
don't repeat what I'm seeking.

So Much From Me

He fills my ear with worthless chatter
fakes seduction with conceit
after spending minutes with him
he wants so much from me.

How things are different
not so much later
my thoughts became him
my heart thinking major.

Easy come, easy go
nights are over
back to the imperfect life
smarter but colder.

I let you and held on
but it's a two way street
other women to choose from
you're not a man according to me.

Tired of giving
bored from wasted time
not asking for many things
someone
who gives back would be fine.

Talks big does nothing
I don't want that anymore
I'm stuck on square one
getting in touch with you is a chore.

It's not working now
determined for a new
outlook on myself and le go
alone I will improve.

Club House

Underneath the kitchen table
I crawl into my club house
I don't feel like adult games right now
but, I am the happiest kid in town.

Want to be untouched by evils
my job is to use my imagination
looking at the world with wide eyes
master my paint creations.

Plans are all last minute
a blanket is the walls and door
not just anybody can come inside
playing on the floor.

So hopeful for tommorow
getting dirty and loud
time pulled the blanket off the table
no more club house.

Satan's Road

Goosebumps emerged from flesh
just from looking at satan's road
sin is obvious
it's a place some still go.

Bewitched by personal gain
I am still bewildered as to why
others see it paved with satisfaction
while I just speed on by.

Broken beer bottles in the dirt
snakes crawling from who knows where
people get down on their bellies
with the rest of them there.

Santan's path may be easy
all i see are flames
leading to damnation
he's not taking my name.

He might wear a disguise
you sit and watch his show
don't ask for an encore, he only does one
for each person. he doesn't work slow.

I am not impressed
by his cheap parlor tricks
the Lord gave me better eyes than that
I'm taking his trip.

Feeling Beautiful

It's been some time
since I've felt beautiful
no time like today
with a full heart and moisturized lips.

Perfumed my skin
until my nose was delighted
by flowers and amber
on top of the softness.

My hair was styled
my heels were high
confident posture
and a dynamite dress.

Enough color on my face
to still observe my soul in there
lips saturated in diamond lipstick
an expensive smile.

The walls could tell stories of me
too confident in the moment
to care of what I said
the conversations were real.

I could paint the picture now
and I'm only in the elevator
with my thoughts drowning out
the boring music.

I'm ready
walking to the car
there's excitement but inner peace
I recognized myself tonight.

MELODY STARR

I checked the mirror once more
things are as they should be
ready to drive someone crazy
I opened the door.

The crowd in good nature
gossip overlapped
I became betrothed to a good man
Who needs a red carpet?

Introductions

The sun gave birth to morning
my eyes opened to a vision
his broad shoulders put me in heaven
my unlonely heart kissed him.

He wanted to know me
in all senses
I've tried his patience
then gave him chances.

I never want him to leave
I want him always beside me
and close to my heart
always inspiring me.

I look at him filled with words
that libraries have never heard
and emotions behind them
that can't fight happiness.

Filling the time together
with our introductions
accomplished fascinations
someday humming love.

Eight Hours

Flowing to sleep
on my way to a dream
if my reflections pause
a night of harmony.

Inhale the inspiration of sixteen hours
hold it as long as I can
I hope the rest won't make it disappear
surrendering to the sand man.

Shut my eyes and ears to trains and planes
eyelids closing slow
nightmares are illusions in the morning
but, so real a few hours ago.

I find my comfort spot
turn off all that occurs
give myself more chances
tommorow I'll have more words.

Try a little more
try a little less
open up my mind
let go of what already left.

Tommorow makes all the difference
I have to refresh
send a prayer to God
this could be the best night's sleep yet.

The Shortest Romance

Your looking for something
you think I acquire
if we put our heads together
we could possibly conspire.

I've paid the price of being hasty
life has done things to me
don't want to write it off
don't wish to take it too seriously.

Eyes look deeply
I hope you can see the strength behind
getting comfortable steadily.
weakness wants to climb.

I'm the quiet girl
some pine to know
I give small and large pieces of me
checking the flow.

I'm half open minded
there are plenty of fish in the sea
mistakes could be waiting tommorow
perchance you'll wish you never looked at me.

Perhaps we will derail
before the road
the shortest romance
ever known.

But not knowing is neccesary
have to play the part
from beggining until whenever
preparation to stop and start.

MELODY STARR

The World's Room

The key is in the house
I'm locking myself out
wildly happy smiles are waiting
and I need some saving.

I smell the rain in advance
only makes my mind more inquiring
out to find an attendant
too much time admiring.

The walls were too thick
old air made me sick
windows made me long more
now thrilled for whats in store.

The sun will show all my colors
portrayed in black and white
I have alot of buildup
release will make the load light.

I feel ready this time
the world is mine
more in me excelling
more stories for telling.

Bouquet Of Flowers

You gave me a bouquet of promise
from your hands to mine
a presumptous moral seduction
and a tasteful incline.

Waking up to the parfumed scent
of a lasting glee
an assurance of no other
these flowers are for me.

We've captured this place
and graduating new heights
my mind dials out your name
your never a long ride.

Love always feels new
and more fresh each slice
showing each other more characters
everyday a great surprise.

I didn't think I had so much to give
it flew out of me like a rushing wind
something told me not to be afraid
had too much to win.

Printed in the United States
By Bookmasters